Horses

Julie Murray

Abdo
I LIKE ANIMALS!
Kids

abdopublishing.com

Published by Abdo Kids, a division of ABDO, PO Box 398166, Minneapolis, Minnesota 55439.
Copyright © 2017 by Abdo Consulting Group, Inc. International copyrights reserved in all countries.
No part of this book may be reproduced in any form without written permission from the publisher.

Printed in the United States of America, North Mankato, Minnesota.

052016

092016

 THIS BOOK CONTAINS
RECYCLED MATERIALS

Photo Credits: iStock, Shutterstock

Production Contributors: Teddy Borth, Jennie Forsberg, Grace Hansen

Design Contributors: Candice Keimig, Dorothy Toth

Cataloging-in-Publication Data

Names: Murray, Julie, author.

Title: Horses / by Julie Murray.

Description: Minneapolis, MN : Abdo Kids, [2017] |Series: I like animals! |
     Includes bibliographical references and index.

Identifiers: LCCN 2015959203 | ISBN 9781680805314 (lib. bdg.) |
     ISBN 9781680805871 (ebook) | ISBN 9781680806434 (Read-to-me ebook)

Subjects: LCSH: Horses--Juvenile literature.

Classification: DDC 636.1--dc23

LC record available at http://lccn.loc.gov/2015959203

Table of Contents

Horses

Most horses live on farms.

Chad rides a horse.

Horses have **manes**.

They also have long tails.

Nikki brushes her horse.

Horses come in many colors.

Tami rides a brown horse.

Horses have strong bodies.

They have four legs.

They can run fast!

Horses have large eyes.

They have pointed ears.

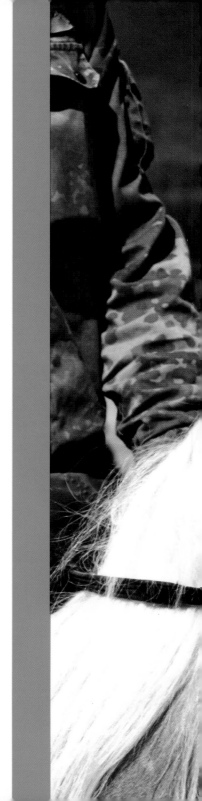

Horses have **hoofs**. Ella cleans her horse's hoofs.

Boy horses are called stallions. Girls are mares. Babies are foals.

stallion

mare

foal

17

Horses eat grass and hay. They like carrots and apples, too!

What do you like

about horses?

Some Kinds of Horses

American Paint

Gypsy

Arabian

Shire

Glossary

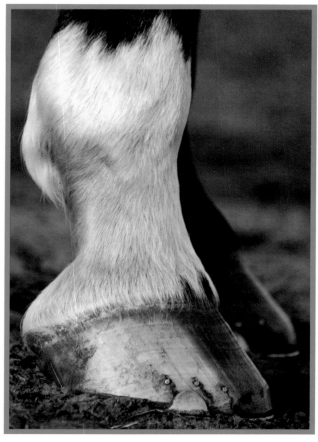

hoof
the hard covering on the foot
of some animals.

mane
long, thick hair growing from
the neck.

Index

abdokids.com

Use this code to log on to abdokids.com and access crafts, games, videos, and more!

Abdo Kids Code:
IHK5314

24